Oxford University Press, Walton Street, Oxford OX2 6DP

Oxford New York Toronto
Delhi Bombay Calcutta Madras Karachi
Petaling Jaya Singapore Hong Kong Tokyo
Nairobi Dar es Salaam Cape Town
Melbourne Auckland

and associated companies in
Beirut Berlin Ibadan Nicosia

Oxford is a trade mark of Oxford University Press

ISBN 0-19-281167-3

© The Trianon Press 1975

First published in 1975 by Oxford University Press
in association with The Trianon Press
125 avenue du Maine, Paris 14e
Reprinted 1985 (twice), 1986, 1988

Library of Congress Catalog Card no. 75-4495

The text was set in Monotype Bembo by
William Clowes, London and by Darantiere, Dijon
The book was designed by Arnold Fawcus

The title-page overleaf is taken from Copy E,
Keynes-Wolf 'Census', which had also been used for
the enlargements of the interlinear decorations in
the Commentary

Printed in Hong Kong

This reproduction in the original size

of William Blake's Illuminated Book

THE MARRIAGE

OF HEAVEN AND HELL

with an Introduction and Commentary

by Sir Geoffrey Keynes

is published by

OXFORD UNIVERSITY PRESS

OXFORD & NEW YORK

in association with The Trianon Press, Paris

Contents and Summary

* * *

Plate 1   [The Title-page]
Sets the scene of the book, introducing the principal participants, the
Angel (Reason) and the Devil (Imagination) uniting in their consum-
mation of the Marriage of Heaven and Hell.

Plate 2   *The Argument*
A prose poem, in which Blake, as 'Rintrah', chastises Society as he
sees it, degenerate and apathetic, devoid of Energy and Imagination,
and welcomes the era of Revolution that was dawning in Europe.

Plate 3
Describes the Swedenborgian attitude of the conventional Good
Angel, sterile and unimaginative, while the Newborn Terror is
being born by Revolution with consequent liberation from restric-
tive morals. Announces Blake's doctrine of Contraries.

Plate 4   *The voice of the Devil*
Blake specifies the three main errors of conventional religion with the
contrary truths in favour of Liberty and Energy, voiced by the Devil,
illustrated by the Good and Evil Angels in contest.

religion) go on a fantastic journey each shewing the other their 'lots in eternity'. The Angel is vanquished and flees.

Plate 21 and upper part of Plate 22
A criticism of the Angel's general attitude based on Reason, mostly second-hand, in the light of Blake's own doctrine of Contraries.

Plates 22–24   A Memorable Fancy
Relates a contest between Blake, who identifies God with Man, and a conventional Angel, who is finally persuaded and becomes Blake's ally. Together they read the Bible of Hell. Heaven and Hell are reconciled.

Plates 25–27   A Song of Liberty
An ode celebrating Revolution and the liberation of the subconscious mind in the triumphal reunion of the Devil and the Angel. Now every living thing becomes holy through Man's equation with God through his Imagination. Tyranny has collapsed and the Artist is free.

Publisher's Note

This book has evolved, like its companion volume *Songs of Innocence and of Experience*, from our work with the William Blake Trust to whom we are again indebted. The Trust's own facsimile, now out of print, was made from the Rosenwald copy, but for this edition it was decided to reproduce a very lovely copy of *The Marriage of Heaven and Hell* in the Fitzwilliam Museum which offered a striking contrast in colour to the Rosenwald volume that we had reproduced in a limited edition, as well as a special challenge to our abilities to make a reproduction, both reasonably accurate and easily accessible to a wide public.

We have used six and seven colours in photo-lithography and made four series of proofs, correcting each from the original in Cambridge. The result, we feel, is as close to the original as can be obtained by a photo-mechanical process. We are most indebted to the Director of the Fitzwilliam, Professor Michael Jaffé, to the former Director, Mr. David Piper, and to their staff who have helped us generously. To Mr. George Rawlings, the University Library photographic specialist, who devoted much time and skill to making an unusually accurate set of ektachromes from which we have worked in Paris, we are especially grateful.

For Sir Geoffrey Keynes this volume has again been a labour of love. Without his advice, encouragement, and patience the project would have foundered. Like him we felt that Blake's message in *The Marriage of Heaven and Hell* was so important and his wisdom so timely that every endeavour should be made to make it as widely available as possible in the form in which Blake intended it to be read.

ARNOLD FAWCUS

Introduction

THE MARRIAGE OF HEAVEN AND HELL holds a unique position among the works presented by Blake in his series of Illuminated Books. It came early in the sequence, being preceded only by the *Songs of Innocence* and *The Book of Thel* and differs from these and from all the other books by being written principally in prose; and it was Blake's first full-scale attempt to present his philosophic message. Blake was primarily a poet, but both his poetry and his prose were concerned with philosophy, often to the dismay of readers of poetry. He was a philosopher-poet, putting Imagination above Reason and so seemed to upset what is usually regarded as the foundation of the doctrines propounded by his predecessors such as Bacon, Newton, and Locke. They placed God above and separate from Man, whereas Blake regarded human imagination as the essential divine quality by which God manifested himself in Man. This was almost equating Man with God and Art with Christianity. Blake had therefore reached the extremity of humanism, an attitude which seemed to his contemporaries, startled by so revolutionary a mode of thought, to be explicable only as a form of insanity. So complete an artist was quite beyond their comprehension.

It is believed that Blake began to compose *The Marriage of Heaven and Hell* in about 1789, when he was already aged 32, having had ten years since emerging from his apprenticeship as an engraver, during which he developed his mental attitudes by thought and reading. His output as poet and pictorial artist had been limited to the *Poetical Sketches* of his adolescence and *Songs of Innocence* and *The Book of Thel* of his young manhood and a few minor books. His flair for effective use of satire had been adumbrated in his high-spirited burlesque, kept only in manuscript and known as *An Island in the Moon*.

As a boy of fourteen he had, according to his own statement, already read, criticized, and rejected the conventional philosophers and their materialistic views of the meaning of human life. He had become, in fact, a mature thinker, while he had by patient experiment and practice evolved a method of presenting his thoughts in the entirely original and attractive form of Illuminated Printing, as unlike the usual form of philosophical treatise as can be conceived. He had rejected from the start any thought of mass production such as is achieved by the ordinary printed page. Everything he produced in the form of poetry, philosophy, or philosophical poetry was to take the form of an attractive work of art made entirely by his own hands without the help of the materialistic society by which he was surrounded. Blake was individualistic to the point of crankiness, but his integrity as an artist was thereby ensured.

During this period of intellectual development Blake had been interested in the writings of Emmanuel Swedenborg, the Swedish visionary theologian, as his annotated copies of some of Swedenborg's books testify. Those which remain today are *Divine Love*, 1788, *Heaven and Hell*, 1789, and *Divine Providence*, 1790. However, Blake soon realized that Swedenborg had more in common with the materialism, which he claimed he had rejected, than with Blake's own turn of thought. Although he continued to value some of Swedenborg's attitudes, he came to regard him as fair game for satire and based the very title of his own philosophical treatise on Swedenborg's *Heaven and Hell*, calling it *The Marriage of Heaven and Hell* and thereby reversing the meaning of the terms 'Heaven' and 'Hell'. Blake's Devil personified energy, which is good; Swedenborg's Angel supported conventional thought and religion, which is bad. Blake was also certainly mocking the passages which Swedenborg had called 'Memorable Relations' with his own 'Memorable Fancies'.

For Swedenborg the spiritual world was in a kind of mechanistic equilibrium quite foreign to Blake's ideal of the creative energy of which man's spiritual life ought to consist. He enunciated this doctrine in the fourth plate of the *Marriage* in its clearest form, calling it 'The voice of the Devil'. On the third plate he had stated the doctrine of Contraries—Attraction and Repulsion, Reason and Energy, Love and Hate. Without these contraries there could be no progression, that is, human thought and life need the stimulus of active and opposing forces to give them creative movement. In the light of this principle Blake gave the qualities, Good and Evil, meanings opposite to their usual acceptation, and in the fourth plate announced in plain terms how the wrong interpretation had arisen, stemming from the conventional moral codes. To him passive acceptance was evil, active opposition was good. This is the key to the meaning of the paradoxes and inversions of which the whole work consists. Angels and Devils change places. Good is Evil. Heaven is Hell. Though freely using satire and paradox, Blake gives in this book some of the most explicit statements of his mental attitudes, which he elaborated in the later Prophetic Books and restated even more clearly in the phrases of the *Laocoön* plate in 1820.

It is important to remember while reading the book that there are two primary features throughout—satire and personal philosophy. Blake is being neither flippant nor too serious; the *Marriage* has much wit and good humour mingled with the expression of deeply felt personal convictions.

★   ★   ★

If 1789 was the year in which *The Marriage of Heaven and Hell* was begun, 1790 was probably the year of its completion. Blake had perfected the technique by which he produced the illuminated pages of his books when he finished his *Songs of Innocence* in 1789. He had mastered the difficult process of making deeply etched copperplates with both text and designs, which could be printed from the surface of the plates without great pressure. This could be done either by a form of colour-printing with an opaque medium or by making a print in coloured ink, which could then be illuminated in water-colours. Lack of understanding of Blake's paradoxical philosophy ensured that the book would not have a wide circulation. Only nine copies of *The Marriage of Heaven and Hell* are known at the present time and it seems unlikely that any copies of so striking and unusual a work of art could have been destroyed. There is a wide variation of colour and detail among these copies and the dating of each copy can only be approximate. In one copy, on plate 3, Blake has put the date 1790 above the first words of the sentence: 'As a new heaven is begun, and it is now thirty-three years since its advent, the Eternal Hell revives'. This ostensibly refers to the New Jerusalem announced by Swedenborg for the year 1757. The Eternal Hell means the revolutions in both France and America and the date refers less obviously to the year of Blake's birth, a convenient coincidence for him, because the 'revival of Hell' depended partly on the composition and publication of Blake's own books. Though it may be assumed that in 1790 the work was well advanced and probably completed, it cannot be established when the first copy was printed, since most do not have a dated watermark in the paper and none has a provenance precise enough to identify it as the first.

*   *   *

The copy of *The Marriage of Heaven and Hell* here reproduced is one of two preserved in the Fitzwilliam Museum, Cambridge. Both are printed in a light red-brown ink and painted with water-colour washes; they were certainly completed late in

Blake's life. The one chosen for reproduction is unique in having the text illuminated in various bright colours, though these do not seem to have any direct relation to the meanings. Blake printed the plates on both sides of the sheet and thus took advantage of the double openings to balance the brilliant colours used. In the reproduction, while preserving the artist's intention, the plates have been printed on one side only, the blank pages thus made available on the verso of the plates being utilized to bring the Commentary into closer relation to the plates discussed.

The leaves have no watermark to help in dating the volume, but it certainly belonged to John Linnell, Blake's friend and patron from 1818 until his death in 1827. A receipt is in existence proving that Linnell paid Blake two guineas for the book in April 1821. It remained in the possession of the Linnell family until the collection was sold at auction in 1918, when it was bought by T. H. Riches, who had married a grand-daughter of Linnell. Mrs. Riches deposited the book in the Fitzwilliam Museum after her husband's death and it became the property of the Museum at her own death in 1950. The other somewhat similar copy has a watermark dated 1825 confirming the late date of both examples, which have a delicacy of execution not seen in any of the others. The second Fitzwilliam copy was reproduced for J. M. Dent in 1927; the present one has never been reproduced before except for two plates included in my *Bibliography of Blake*, published in 1921 for the Grolier Club of New York.

A feature of the twenty-seven plates constituting all the nine extant copies of the book are the numerous tiny decorations etched by Blake in the spaces between the lines of text. A detailed study of these was made by D. V. Erdman in a volume of *Essays on Blake* published by the Clarendon Press, Oxford, in 1973; and this has afforded help in compiling the description and commentary printed here. These pictorial and often witty glosses on the text illustrate in the main the relations between the Body and the Soul, but their interpretation is not always easy and must be regarded as sometimes conjectural. They are better seen in the earlier copies of the book, being printed in a darker ink. The lighter printing of the present copy makes them sometimes indistinct, but the descriptions have been made with reference to an early copy in my own possession and some have been enlarged and reproduced from the darker copy. It is hoped that this will help readers to appreciate their interest.

Many other writers, from A. C. Swinburne in 1868 onwards, have offered interpretations of *The Marriage of Heaven and Hell*, sometimes from special standpoints, such as Erdman in *Prophet against Empire*, 1969, finding expression of political insights in unlikely places, or Fabri-Tabrizi in *The 'Heaven' and 'Hell' of William Blake*, 1973, detecting references to Swedenborg's *Heaven and Hell* in almost every sentence. The present commentary on the text and illustrations seeks to give the book a simpler provenance, keeping the meaning related as closely as possible to Blake's personal standpoint. This may be criticized as superficial, but it helps to keep the discussion within bounds.

It is worth remarking that much of the script shows what may be interpreted as bad 'register' in the printing. In fact the appearance is usually owing to the fact that Blake has done much of the colouring by pen, and has not always covered accurately the printed impression. In this and in all respects the reproduction is most satisfactory.

GEOFFREY KEYNES

THE MARRIAGE OF HEAVEN AND HELL

THE ARGUMENT

Plate 2

Rintrah roars & shakes his fires in the burden'd air;
Hungry clouds swag on the deep.

Once meek, and in a perilous path,
The just man kept his course along
The vale of death.
Roses are planted where thorns grow,
And on the barren heath
Sing the honey bees.

Then the perilous path was planted:
And a river and a spring
On every cliff and tomb:
And on the bleached bones
Red clay brought forth.

Till the villain left the paths of ease,
To walk in perilous paths, and drive
The just man into barren climes.

Now the sneaking serpent walks
In mild humility,
And the just man rages in the wilds
Where lions roam.

Rintrah roars & shakes his fires in the burden'd air;
Hungry clouds swag on the deep.

Plate 3

As a new heaven is begun, and it is now thirty-three years since its
advent: the Eternal Hell revives. And lo! Swedenborg is the Angel
sitting at the tomb: his writings are the linen clothes folded up. Now
is the dominion of Edom, & the return of Adam into Paradise; see
Isaiah xxxiv & xxxv Chap:

Without Contraries is no progression. Attraction and Repulsion, Reason and Energy, Love and Hate, are necessary to Human existence.

From these contraries spring what the religious call Good & Evil. Good is the passive that obeys Reason. Evil is the active springing from Energy.

Good is Heaven. Evil is Hell.

THE VOICE OF THE DEVIL

Plate 4

All Bibles or sacred codes have been the causes of the following Errors:

1. That Man has two real existing principles: Viz: a Body & a Soul.

2. That Energy, call'd Evil, is alone from the Body, & that Reason, call'd Good, is alone from the Soul.

3. That God will torment Man in Eternity for following his Energies.

But the following Contraries to these are True:

1. Man has no Body distinct from his Soul; for that call'd Body is a portion of Soul discern'd by the five Senses, the chief inlets of Soul in this age.

2. Energy is the only life and is from the Body and Reason is the bound or outward circumference of Energy.

3. Energy is Eternal Delight.

Plates 5-6

Those who restrain desire, do so because theirs is weak enough to be restrained; and the restrainer or Reason usurps its place & governs the unwilling.

And being restrain'd, it by degrees becomes passive, till it is only the shadow of desire.

The history of this is written in Paradise Lost, & the Governor or Reason is call'd Messiah.

And the original Archangel, or possessor of the command of the heavenly host, is call'd the Devil or Satan, and his children are call'd Sin & Death.

But in the Book of Job, Milton's Messiah is call'd Satan.

For this history has been adopted by both parties.

It indeed appear'd to Reason as if Desire was cast out, but the Devil's account is, that the Messiah fell, & formed a heaven of what he stole from the Abyss.

This is shewn in the Gospel, where he prays to the Father to send the comforter, or Desire, that Reason may have Ideas to build on, the Jehovah of the Bible being no other than [the Devil *del.*] he who dwells in flaming fire.

Know that after Christ's death, he became Jehovah.

But in Milton, the Father is Destiny, the Son, a Ratio of the five senses, & the Holy-ghost, Vacuum!

Note: The reason Milton wrote in fetters when he wrote of Angels & God, and at liberty when of Devils & Hell, is because he was a true Poet and of the Devil's party without knowing it.

A MEMORABLE FANCY

Plates 6-7

As I was walking among the fires of hell, delighted with the enjoyments of Genius, which to Angels look like torment and insanity, I collected some of their Proverbs; thinking that as the sayings used in a nation mark its character, so the Proverbs of Hell shew the nature of Infernal wisdom better than any description of buildings or garments.

When I came home: on the abyss of the five senses, where a flat sided steep frowns over the present world, I saw a mighty Devil folded in black clouds, hovering on the sides of the rock, with corroding fires he wrote the following sentence now percieved by the minds of men, & read by them on earth:

How do you know but ev'ry Bird that cuts the airy way,
Is an immense world of delight, clos'd by your senses five?

PROVERBS OF HELL

Plates 7-10

In seed time learn, in harvest teach, in winter enjoy.
Drive your cart and your plow over the bones of the dead.

The road of excess leads to the palace of wisdom.

Prudence is a rich ugly old maid courted by Incapacity.

He who desires but acts not, breeds pestilence.

The cut worm forgives the plow.

Dip him in the river who loves water.

A fool sees not the same tree that a wise man sees.

He whose face gives no light, shall never become a star.

Eternity is in love with the productions of time.

The busy bee has no time for sorrow.

The hours of folly are measur'd by the clock; but of wisdom, no clock can measure.

All wholsom food is caught without a net or a trap.

Bring out number, weight & measure in a year of dearth.

No bird soars too high, if he soars with his own wings.

A dead body revenges not injuries.

The most sublime act is to set another before you.

If the fool would persist in his folly he would become wise.

Folly is the cloke of knavery.

Shame is Pride's cloke.

Prisons are built with stones of Law, Brothels with bricks of Religion.

The pride of the peacock is the glory of God.

The lust of the goat is the bounty of God.

The wrath of the lion is the wisdom of God.

The nakedness of woman is the work of God.

Excess of sorrow laughs. Excess of joy weeps.

The roaring of lions, the howling of wolves, the raging of the stormy sea, and the destructive sword, are portions of eternity too great for the eye of man.

The fox condemns the trap, not himself.

Joys impregnate. Sorrows bring forth.

Let man wear the fell of the lion, woman the fleece of the sheep.

The bird a nest, the spider a web, man friendship.

The selfish smiling fool, & the sullen, frowning fool shall be both thought wise, that they may be a rod.

What is now proved was once only imagin'd.

The rat, the mouse, the fox, the rabbet watch the roots; the lion, the tyger, the horse, the elephant, watch the fruits.

The cistern contains : the fountain overflows.

One thought fills immensity.

Always be ready to speak your mind, and a base man will avoid you.

Every thing possible to be believ'd is an image of truth.

The eagle never lost so much time, as when he submitted to learn of the crow.

— The fox provides for himself, but God provides for the lion.

Think in the morning. Act in the noon. Eat in the evening. Sleep in the night.

He who has suffer'd you to impose on him knows you.

As the plow follows words, so God rewards prayers.

The tygers of wrath are wiser than the horses of instruction.

Expect poison from the standing water.

You never know what is enough unless you know what is more than enough.

Listen to the fool's reproach! it is a kingly title!

The eyes of fire, the nostrils of air, the mouth of water, the beard of earth.

The weak in courage is strong in cunning.

The apple tree never asks the beech how he shall grow; nor the lion, the horse, how he shall take his prey.

The thankful reciever bears a plentiful harvest.

If others had not been foolish, we should be so.

The soul of sweet delight can never be defil'd.

When thou seest an Eagle, thou seest a portion of Genius; lift up thy head!

As the catterpiller chooses the fairest leaves to lay her eggs on, so the priest lays his curse on the fairest joys.

To create a little flower is the labour of ages.

Damn braces : Bless relaxes.

The best wine is the oldest, the best water the newest.

Prayers plow not! Praises reap not!

Joys laugh not! Sorrows weep not!

— The head Sublime, the heart Pathos, the genitals Beauty, the hands & feet Proportion.

As the air to a bird or the sea to a fish, so is contempt to the contemptible.

The crow wish'd every thing was black, the owl that every thing was white.

Exuberance is Beauty.

If the lion was advised by the fox, he would be cunning.

Improve[me]nt makes strait roads; but the crooked roads without Improvement are roads of Genius.

Sooner murder an infant in its cradle than nurse unacted desires.

Where man is not, nature is barren.

Truth can never be told so as to be understood, and not be believ'd.

Enough! or Too much.

Plate 11

The ancient Poets animated all sensible objects with Gods or Geniuses, calling them by the names and adorning them with the properties of woods, rivers, mountains, lakes, cities, nations, and whatever their enlarged & numerous senses could percieve.

And particularly they studied the genius of each city & country, placing it under its mental deity;

Till a system was formed, which some took advantage of, & enslav'd the vulgar by attempting to realize or abstract the mental deities from their objects: thus began Priesthood;

Choosing forms of worship from poetic tales.

And at length they pronounc'd that the Gods had order'd such things.

Thus men forgot that All deities reside in the human breast.

A MEMORABLE FANCY

Plates 12–13

The Prophets Isaiah and Ezekiel dined with me, and I asked them how they dared so roundly to assert that God spoke to them; and whether they did not think at the time that they would be misunderstood, & so be the cause of imposition.

Isaiah answer'd: 'I saw no God, nor heard any, in a finite organical perception; but my senses discover'd the infinite in every thing, and as I was then perswaded, & remain confirm'd, that the voice of honest indignation is the voice of God, I cared not for consequences, but wrote.'

Then I asked: 'does a firm perswasion that a thing is so, make it so?'

He replied: 'All poets believe that it does, & in ages of imagination this firm perswasion removed mountains; but many are not capable of a firm perswasion of any thing.'

Then Ezekiel said: 'The philosophy of the east taught the first principles of human perception: some nations held one principle for the origin, & some another: we of Israel taught that the Poetic Genius (as you now call it) was the first principle and all the others merely derivative, which was the cause of our despising the Priests & Philosophers of other countries, and prophecying that all Gods would at last be proved to originate in ours & to be the tributaries of the Poetic Genius; it was this that our great poet King David desired so fervently & invokes so pathetic'ly, saying by this he conquers enemies & governs kingdoms; and we so loved our God, that we cursed in his name all the deities of surrounding nations, and asserted that they had rebelled; from these opinions the vulgar came to think that all nations would at last be subject to the jews.'

'This,' said he, 'like all firm perswasions, is come to pass; for all nations believe the jews' code and worship the jews' god, and what greater subjection can be?'

I heard this with some wonder, & must confess my own conviction. After dinner I ask'd Isaiah to favour the world with his lost works; he said none of equal value was lost. Ezekiel said the same of his.

I also asked Isaiah what made him go naked and barefoot three years? he answer'd: 'the same that made our friend Diogenes, the Grecian.'

I then asked Ezekiel why he eat dung, & lay so long on his right & left side? he answer'd, 'the desire of raising other men into a perception of the infinite: this the North American tribes practise, & is he honest who resists his genius or conscience only for the sake of present ease or gratification?'

Plate 14

The ancient tradition that the world will be consumed in fire at the end of six thousand years is true, as I have heard from Hell.

For the cherub with his flaming sword is hereby commanded to leave his guard at tree of life; and when he does, the whole creation will be consumed and appear infinite and holy, whereas it now appears finite & corrupt.

This will come to pass by an improvement of sensual enjoyment.

But first the notion that man has a body distinct from his soul is to be expunged; this I shall do by printing in the infernal method, by corrosives, which in Hell are salutary and medicinal, melting apparent surfaces away, and displaying the infinite which was hid.

If the doors of perception were cleansed every thing would appear to man as it is, Infinite.

For man has closed himself up, till he sees all things thro' narrow chinks of his cavern.

A MEMORABLE FANCY

Plate 15

I was in a Printing house in Hell & saw the method in which knowledge is transmitted from generation to generation.

In the first chamber was a Dragon-Man, clearing away the rubbish from a cave's mouth; within, a number of Dragons were hollowing the cave.

In the second chamber was a Viper folding round the rock & the cave, and others adorning it with gold, silver and precious stones.

In the third chamber was an Eagle with wings and feathers of air: he caused the inside of the cave to be infinite; around were numbers of Eagle-like men, who built palaces in the immense cliffs.

In the fourth chamber were Lions of flaming fire, raging around & melting the metals into living fluids.

In the fifth chamber were Unnam'd forms, which cast the metals into the expanse.

There they were reciev'd by Men who occupied the sixth chamber, and took the forms of books & were arranged in libraries.

Plates 16–17

The Giants who formed this world into its sensual existence and now seem to live in it in chains, are in truth the causes of its life & the sources of all activity; but the chains are the cunning of weak and tame minds which have power to resist energy, according to the proverb, the weak in courage is strong in cunning.

Thus one portion of being is the Prolific, the other the Devouring: to the devourer it seems as if the producer was in his chains; but it is not so, he only takes portions of existence and fancies that the whole.

But the Prolific would cease to be Prolific unless the Devourer, as a sea, recieved the excess of his delights.

Some will say: 'Is not God alone the Prolific?' I answer: 'God only Acts & Is, in existing beings or Men.'

These two classes of men are always upon earth, & they should be enemies: whoever tries to reconcile them seeks to destroy existence.

Religion is an endeavour to reconcile the two.

Note: Jesus Christ did not wish to unite, but to seperate them, as in the Parable of sheep and goats! & he says: 'I came not to send Peace, but a Sword.'

Messiah or Satan or Tempter was formerly thought to be one of the Antediluvians who are our Energies.

A MEMORABLE FANCY

Plates 17-20

An Angel came to me and said: 'O pitiable foolish young man! O horrible! O dreadful state! consider the hot burning dungeon thou art preparing for thyself to all eternity, to which thou art going in such career.'

I said: 'perhaps you will be willing to shew me my eternal lot & we will contemplate together upon it and see whether your lot or mine is most desirable.'

So he took me thro' a stable & thro' a church & down into the church vault, at the end of which was a mill: thro' the mill we went, and came to a cave: down the winding cavern we groped our tedious way, till a void boundless as a nether sky appear'd beneath us, & we held by the roots of trees and hung over this immensity; but I said: 'if you please, we will commit ourselves to this void, and see whether providence is here also: if you will not, I will?' but he answer'd: 'do not presume, O young-man, but as we here remain, behold thy lot which will soon appear when the darkness passes away.'

So I remain'd with him, sitting in the twisted root of an oak; he was suspended in a fungus, which hung with the head downward into the deep.

By degrees we beheld the infinite Abyss, fiery as the smoke of a burning city; beneath us, at an immense distance, was the sun, black but shining; round it were fiery tracks on which revolv'd vast spiders, crawling after their prey, which flew, or rather swum, in the infinite deep, in the most terrific shapes of animals sprung from corruption; & the air was full of them, & seem'd composed of them: these are Devils, and are called Powers of the air. I now asked my companion which was my eternal lot? he said: 'between the black & white spiders.'

But now, from between the black & white spiders, a cloud and fire burst and rolled thro' the deep, black'ning all beneath, so that the nether deep grew black as a sea, & rolled with a terrible noise; beneath us was nothing now to be seen but a black tempest, till looking east between the clouds & the waves, we saw a cataract of blood mixed with fire, and not many stones' throw from us appear'd and sunk again the scaly fold of a monstrous serpent; at last, to the east, distant about three degrees, appear'd a fiery crest above the waves; slowly it reared like a ridge of golden rocks, till we discover'd two globes of crimson fire, from which the sea fled away in clouds of smoke; and now we saw it was the head of Leviathan; his forehead was divided into streaks of green & purple like those on a tyger's forehead: soon we saw his mouth & red gills hang just above the raging foam, tinging the black deep with beams of blood, advancing toward us with all the fury of a spiritual existence.

My friend the Angel climb'd up from his station into the mill; I remain'd alone; & then this appearance was no more, but I found myself sitting on a pleasant bank beside a river by moonlight, hearing a harper, who sung to the harp; & his theme was: 'The man who never alters his opinion is like standing water, & breeds reptiles of the mind.'

But I arose and sought for the mill, & there I found my Angel, who, surprised, asked me how I escaped?

I answer'd: 'All that we saw was owing to your metaphysics; for when you ran away, I found myself on a bank by moonlight hearing a harper. But now we have seen my eternal lot, shall I shew you yours?' he laugh'd at my proposal; but I by force suddenly caught him in my arms, & flew westerly thro' the night, till we were elevated above the earth's shadow; then I flung myself with him directly into the body of the sun; here I clothed myself in white, & taking in my hand Swedenborg's volumes, sunk from the glorious clime, and passed all the planets till we came to saturn: here I staid to rest, & then leap'd into the void between saturn & the fixed stars.

'Here,' said I, 'is your lot, in this space, if space it may be call'd.' Soon we saw the stable and the church, & I took him to the altar and open'd the Bible, and lo! it was a deep pit, into which I descended, driving the Angel before me; soon we saw seven houses of brick; one we enter'd; in it were a number of monkeys, baboons, & all of that species, chain'd by the middle, grinning and snatching at one another, but witheld by the shortness of their chains: however, I saw that they sometimes grew numerous, and then the weak were caught by the strong, and with a grinning aspect, first coupled with, & then devour'd, by plucking off first one limb and then another, till the body was left a helpless trunk; this, after grinning & kissing it with seeming fondness, they devour'd too; and here & there I saw one savourily picking the flesh off of his own tail; as the stench terribly annoy'd us both, we went into the mill, & I in my hand brought the skeleton of a body, which in the mill was Aristotle's Analytics.

So the Angel said: 'thy phantasy has imposed upon me, & thou oughtest to be ashamed.'

I answer'd: 'we impose on one another, & it is but lost time to converse with you whose works are only Analytics.'

Opposition is true Friendship.

Plates 21-22

I have always found that Angels have the vanity to speak of themselves as the only wise; this they do with a confident insolence sprouting from systematic reasoning.

Thus Swedenborg boasts that what he writes is new; tho' it is only the Contents or Index of already publish'd books.

A man carried a monkey about for a shew, & because he was a little wiser than the monkey, grew vain, and conciev'd himself as much wiser than seven men. It is so with Swedenborg: he shews the folly of churches & exposes hypocrites, till he imagines that all are religious, & himself the single one on earth that ever broke a net.

Now hear a plain fact: Swedenborg has not written one new truth. Now hear another: he has written all the old falshoods.

And now hear the reason. He conversed with Angels who are all religious, & conversed not with Devils who all hate religion, for he was incapable thro' his conceited notions.

Thus Swedenborg's writings are a recapitulation of all superficial opinions, and an analysis of the more sublime, but no further.

Have now another plain fact. Any man of mechanical talents may, from the writings of Paracelsus or Jacob Behmen, produce ten thousand volumes of equal value with Swedenborg's, and from those of Dante or Shakespear an infinite number.

But when he has done this, let him not say that he knows better than his master, for he only holds a candle in sunshine.

A MEMORABLE FANCY

Plates 22-24

Once I saw a Devil in a flame of fire, who arose before an Angel that sat on a cloud, and the Devil utter'd these words:

'The worship of God is: Honouring his gifts in other men, each according to his genius, and loving the greatest men best: those who envy or calumniate great men hate God; for there is no other God.'

The Angel hearing this became almost blue, but mastering himself he grew yellow, & at last white, pink, & smiling, and then replied:

'Thou Idolater. is not God One? & is not he visible in Jesus Christ? and has not Jesus Christ given his sanction to the law of ten commandments, and are not all other men fools, sinners, & nothings?'

The Devil answer'd: 'bray a fool in a morter with wheat, yet shall not his folly be beaten out of him; if Jesus Christ is the greatest man, you ought to love him in the greatest degree; now hear how he has given his sanction to the law of ten commandments: did he not mock at the sabbath, and so mock the sabbath's God? murder those who were murder'd because of him? turn away the law from the woman taken in adultery? steal the labor of others to support him? bear false witness when he omitted making a defence before Pilate? covet when he pray'd for his disciples, and when he bid them shake off the dust of their feet against such as refused to lodge them? I tell you, no virtue can exist without breaking these ten commandments. Jesus was all virtue, and acted from impulse, not from rules.'

When he had so spoken, I beheld the Angel, who stretched out his arms, embracing the flame of fire, & he was consumed and arose as Elijah.

Note: This Angel, who is now become a Devil, is my particular friend; we often read the Bible together in its infernal or diabolical sense, which the world shall have if they behave well.

I have also The Bible of Hell, which the world shall have whether they will or no.

One Law for the Lion & Ox is Oppression.

A SONG OF LIBERTY

Plates 25-27

1. The Eternal Female groan'd! it was heard over all the Earth.
2. Albion's coast is sick silent; the American meadows faint!
3. Shadows of Prophecy shiver along by the lakes and the rivers and mutter across the ocean: France, rend down thy dungeon;
4. Golden Spain, burst the barriers of old Rome;
5. Cast thy keys, O Rome, into the deep down falling, even to eternity down falling,
6. And weep [and bow thy reverend locks.[1]]
7. In her trembling hands she took the new born terror, howling;
8. On those infinite mountains of light, now barr'd out by the atlantic sea, the new born fire stood before the starry king!
9. Flag'd with grey brow'd snows and thunderous visages, the jealous wings wav'd over the deep.
10. The speary hand burned aloft, unbuckled was the shield; forth went the hand of jealousy among the flaming hair, and hurl'd the new born wonder thro' the starry night.
11. The fire, the fire is falling!

[1] The last five words afterwards erased from the plate.

12. Look up! look up! O citizen of London, enlarge thy countenance: O Jew, leave counting gold! return to thy oil and wine. O African! black African! (go, winged thought, widen his forehead.)

13. The fiery limbs, the flaming hair, shot like the sinking sun into the western sea.

14. Wak'd from his eternal sleep, the hoary element roaring fled away:

15. Down rush'd, beating his wings in vain, the jealous king; his grey brow'd councellors, thunderous warriors, curl'd veterans, among helms, and shields, and chariots, horses, elephants: banners, castles, slings, and rocks,

16. Falling, rushing, ruining! buried in the ruins, on Urthona's dens;

17. All night beneath the ruins, then, their sullen flames faded, emerge round the gloomy King.

18. With thunder and fire, leading his starry hosts thro' the waste wilderness, he promulgates his ten commands, glancing his beamy eyelids over the deep in dark dismay,

19. Where the son of fire in his eastern cloud, while the morning plumes her golden breast,

20. Spurning the clouds written with curses, stamps the stony law to dust, loosing the eternal horses from the dens of night, crying:

Empire is no more! and now the lion & wolf shall cease.

Chorus

Let the Priests of the Raven of dawn, no longer in deadly black, with hoarse note curse the sons of joy. Nor his accepted brethren, whom, tyrant, he calls free: lay the bound or build the roof. Nor pale religious letchery call that virginity that wishes but acts not!

For every thing that lives is Holy.

Blake's spelling, use of capitals, and abbreviations have been followed as in his etched plates. His punctuation, however, was modified for the sake of clarity in The Complete Writings *of William Blake, edited by Geoffrey Keynes (Nonesuch Press, 1957); and this has, with some exceptions, been followed here. Certain lines have been printed in larger type to follow Blake's emphasis.*

Plate 1   THE TITLE-PAGE

The first page carries the title of the book and sets the scene, introducing the principal participants.

About a third of the distance from the upper margin of the design is the surface of the nether world in which the drama is enacted. On this level, beneath the leafless branches of two trees representing 'material existence', are four people; two are walking hand in hand towards the other two, one being a man playing a musical instrument—that is, an Orphic or erotic figure, who kneels before a woman reclining at the foot of a tree. Above them a number of birds soar upwards. Soaring birds, representing the play of man's free imagination, are a recurrent feature of the decoration in the book.

The word MARRIAGE is inscribed in swash capitals, as if to emphasize an achievement, in contrast with the stiff formality of the words HEAVEN and HELL below. On the left, within the abyss beneath, are the flames of Hell streaming out towards the clouds of Heaven. Borne up on these antagonistic, or contrasted, elements are stretched the nude figures of Devil and Angel embracing face to face. Carried up on the flames of Hell towards the clouds are several embracing couples and single figures, shewing how the energy of Hell will impregnate with life the sterile passivity of Heaven and thus anticipating the final sentence of the book:

For every thing that lives is Holy.

'Life' meant to Blake liveliness and creativity, the product of artistic energy, celebrated in the sentences, 'Energy is Eternal Delight' and 'Exuberance is Beauty'. The design illustrates the uniting of the Soul and the Body, the Angel and the Devil in their consummation of the Marriage of Heaven and Hell.

Plate 2   THE ARGUMENT

In the first line we are told that 'Rintrah roars & shakes his fires', thus introducing one of the few personifications of abstract ideas to be found in this book. 'Rintrah' may be understood as 'Wrath', the wrath of the poet-prophet, Blake himself, predicting the results of the era of revolution which was dawning in Europe and America.

The text is almost free verse rather than prose. It describes how the 'just man', the original inhabitant of Paradise, was following 'the perilous path' of true holiness through this world, 'the vale of death'. Then 'the sneaking serpent', the hypocritical imitator of the 'just man', enters in seeming humility and drives him raging into 'the barren climes' of the arbitrary codes of morality, where roam the lions, guardians of the passive lambs, thereby producing the sterile society which was to be chastised by Blake's 'Hungry clouds' in the atmosphere created by the French and American revolutions.

The general idea of the illustrative decoration of the page had been used in the plate of 'The Ecchoing Green' in *Songs of Innocence*, 1789, and was to be used again with variations in an illustration to Gray's 'Ode on a distant prospect of Eton College', 1797 (pl. 5). In these it was comparatively simple, shewing the progress of a child from Innocence to Experience, or sexual maturity, with a boy in the Tree of Life handing down to a girl below, in *Songs of Innocence*, a large bunch of the Grapes of Ecstasy, a symbol of sexuality. In the present context it is not so simple, though it has often been supposed to have very much the same meaning. This view, however, is not tenable. The upper figure among the branches of the Tree of Life is clearly a girl in a flowing robe and the two touching hands are empty. The appearance of grapes, which would in any case be covered by the giving hand, is due to the presence of a leaf behind it. The scene is one of sterility, emphasized by the conspicuously barren vine beside the lower girl, with its tendrils floating uselessly in the wind. The group of apathetic figures on the ground to the left is consistent with this. The rather plump boy lying in the foreground is overshadowed by two vegetable symbols of the organ of generation in its flaccid state, reminiscent of the illustration for 'The Blossom' in *Songs of Innocence*. Each of these is directed ineffectually towards the two naked girls lying nearby. This state of sterility illustrates the 'barren

The Argument.

Rintrah roars & shakes his fires in the burdend air;
Hungry clouds swag on the deep

Once meek, and in a perilous path,
The just man kept his course along
The vale of death.
Roses are planted where thorns grow,
And on the barren heath
Sing the honey bees.

Then the perilous path was planted;
And a river, and a spring
On every cliff and tomb;
And on the bleached bones
Red clay brought forth.

Till the villain left the paths of ease,
To walk in perilous paths, and drive
The just man into barren climes.

Now the sneaking serpent walks
In mild humility.
And the just man rages in the wilds
Where lions roam.

Rintrah roars & shakes his fires in the
burdend air;
Hungry clouds swag on the deep.

As a new heaven is begun, and it is now thir-
ty-three years since its advent: the Eternal Hell
revives. And lo! Swedenborg is the Angel sitting
at the tomb; his writings are the linen clothes folded
up. Now is the dominion of Edom, & the return of
Adam into Paradise; see Isaiah XXXIV & XXXV Chap:
Without **Contraries** is no progression. Attraction
and Repulsion, Reason and Energy, Love and
Hate, are necessary to **Human** existence.
From these contraries spring what the religious call
Good & Evil. Good is the passive that obeys Reason
Evil is the active springing from Energy.
Good is Heaven. Evil is Hell.

Plate 2 (cont.)

climes' of a society devoid of creative energy and imagination, the object of Rintrah's wrath in the accompanying text.

Plate 3

The first line, 'As a new heaven is begun. . .', celebrates the year 1757, as already explained in the introductory remarks, implicating both Swedenborg and Blake himself. In the third line Swedenborg is the 'good' and passive Angel sitting by the tomb of Christ, crucified at the age of thirty-three. The grave clothes of folded linen represent Swedenborg's writings containing the false systems he has created in his prophecy of the Last Judgement. This has resulted in the dominion of Edom, that is, Esau, the honest man, who has triumphed over his crafty brother Jacob, and Adam has returned to Paradise. Isaiah's chapters 34 and 35 prophesied the triumph of Christ's kingdom over the wicked with forgiveness of sins. The return of Adam to Paradise was no part of any prophecy, but Blake's view of Man as the imaginative creator of art would justify his restoration to happiness and the liberation of the 'just man' of the previous page.

In the next seven lines Blake states his system of Contraries already explained. Through these the new freedom will be won.

The design at the top shews the liberated soul rejoicing in the flames of Hell. Below, a woman is giving birth to a child, which emerges from the womb with its arms raised in greeting. Running away from her is a young man closely resembling the running figure of Los, the poet, in flames, shewn on plate 3 of *The Book of Urizen*, 1794. Floating effortlessly beside him is a girl, kissing him as they go. None of these personifications is named in the text, but the scene suggests that the subject is Enitharmon giving birth to Orc, the Newborn Terror, the spirit of Revolution, with Los and his consort carrying forward the sexual emancipation of the new era.

There are several small interlinear symbols. Above the words, 'As a new heaven is begun', is a floating female figure; below them is a soaring bird. Above 'Adam' is a floating male figure. Below the words 'Love and Hate', at the end of the eighth line, two figures, body and soul, are united, standing together hand in hand on Hogarth's double-curved 'Line of Beauty'.

Plate 4   THE VOICE OF THE DEVIL

This plate contains two series of sentences each numbered 1-3, the second set answering the first. The first three are the errors propagated by 'Bibles or sacred codes'; the first two, with their contraries, need no explanation. The third error, 'That God will torment Man in Eternity for following his Energies', is negatived by the words 'Energy is Eternal Delight', and by Blake's belief in the fundamental doctrine of the forgiveness of sins. The scene depicted below resembles the later colour-print called by Blake 'The Good and Evil Angels', though reversed. Both figures are male. The one on the right, rushing out of the enveloping flames of Hell, can only be Blake's Devil, Bodily Energy, striving to rescue the Newborn Terror from the clutching arms of the Good Angel, or Restraint. They are hovering over the rippling waves of the Sea of Time and Space, illuminated by the Sun of Freedom, but the Devil of Energy is fettered by his ankle so that he cannot move, indicating that the group illustrates the 'Errors' of the upper half of the plate, particularly the third, that the energetic man will be in eternal torment.

The interlinear decorations are numerous. At the top, three trumpeters are voicing the Devil's list of errors, the notes of the trumpets being represented by various menacing vegetable and animal symbols. On the second line float a woman and a child, touching hands. On the fourth line is a figure flying away from another one reclining on a curved vegetable surface, that is, the soul leaving the body, which then becomes 'vegetable', or materialistic. On the seventh line, first the soul seeks to rouse the body on his vegetable bed; then he rises from it to re-unite with the soul by joining hands. To the right of these are three figures huddled together on the ground, probably Reasoners, or Materialists, with vegetables sprouting on either side of them. On the ninth line is a free animal flinging up its heels, but ignored by two children facing one another. Beyond them is a man directing a child to look at a quietly

grazing ox, both being symbols of good Angels curbing natural energies. Following the fourteenth line is a series of figures: first the

The voice of the
Devil

All Bibles or sacred codes. have been
the causes of the following Errors.
1. That Man has two real existing princi-
ples Viz: a Body & a Soul.
2. That Energy. call'd Evil. is alone from the
Body. & that Reason. call'd Good. is alone from
the Soul
3. That God will torment Man in Eternity
for following his Energies.
But the following Contraries to these are True
1. Man has no Body distinct from his Soul
for that call'd Body is a portion of Soul discern'd
by the five Senses. the chief inlets of Soul in this
age
2. Energy is the only life and is from the Body
and Reason is the bound or outward circumference
of Energy.
3. Energy is Eternal Delight

Those who restrain desire, do so because theirs
is weak enough to be restrained; and the restrainer or
Reason usurps its place & governs the unwilling.

And being restraind it by degrees becomes passive
till it is only the shadow of desire.

The history of this is written in Paradise Lost. & the
Governor or Reason is calld Messiah.

And the original Archangel or possessor of the com-
mand of the heavenly host, is calld the Devil or Satan
and his children are calld Sin & Death

But in the Book of Job Miltons Messiah is calld
Satan.

For this history has been adopted by both parties

It indeed appeard to Reason as if Desire was
cast out. but the Devils account is that the Messi-

Plate 4 (cont.)

body and soul springing to reunion, the body's vegetable bed having turned into the Line of Beauty; beyond them is a man, presumably deprived of his sense of sight, led by a dog; he is followed by another blindly groping after him, followed in turn by a groping inanimate

shape. Finally, after the end of the second Truth, is a group recalling Blake's colour-printed design of Joseph of Arimathea preaching to the inhabitants of Britain, with his thorn staff planted before him in the ground. He is preaching Christianity, that is artistic energy, to the

people. Behind Joseph is a split tree with a fallen branch barring the way to a horse pulling a Reasoner, seated in a bath-chair.

Plate 5 and upper part of Plate 6

These plates continue the argument concerning the superiority of Energy to Reason and Restraint, beginning with the paradox that weakness is evil, since Reason comes to govern those without enough will of their own. Blake supports this thesis by quoting Milton's *Paradise Lost*, with a side glance at *The Book of Job*, concluding that 'Milton wrote in fetters when he wrote of Angels & God, and at liberty when of Devils & Hell.' He had created a Satan endowed with energy and fire, more attractive to the perceptive reader than his God, who was Destiny, an inescapable despot. His Son had become an uninteresting abstraction, or 'Ratio', derived from the senses; the Holy Ghost, because ignored by Milton, was 'Vacuum'. Milton was therefore 'a true Poet and of the Devil's party without knowing it'.

The design occupying the upper half of plate 5 illustrates the third error, continuing the graphic story begun on the previous page: 'That God will torment Man in Eternity for following his Energies.' The energetic man (whether Blake's Orc, Milton's Lucifer, or

Ovid's Phaethon) is represented as a naked youth falling headlong into flames with his sword, horse, saddle-cloth, and chariot, the last shown only as a broken wheel. In other copies of the book there is also a glowing red orb (Mars) falling on the left, with another, shewn here, smaller and paler (perhaps a moon) falling near the horse's head. Some of this is described in the later book, *America*, plates 4 and 5, in a vision of the Terror, that is, the American revolution.

The first decoration on plate 5, following the word 'unwilling', seems to be the fallen figure of a 'weak and unwilling' man. After 'shadow of desire' on line 5 the same man is lying in the shadow of vegetation and has almost disappeared. On line 7, under the words 'Paradise Lost', there is a reclining figure, perhaps Milton himself, faced by another figure who is holding what appears to be a huge pair of compasses, symbol of the Governor, or Reason, typified

elsewhere by Newton with his compasses. At the end of the tenth line is a winged dragon with a twisted tail, a conflation, according to D.V. Erdman, of the eagle and viper on a later page. On the fourth line from the foot of the page the name 'Satan' is followed by a serpent, Milton's symbol for the Tempter.

Plate 6 and upper part of Plate 7   A MEMORABLE FANCY

There are no major illustrations on this plate. Below the first line, carrying on from plate 5, is an illustrative strip which is difficult to understand. It appears to be one human figure eagerly offering some object to another with arms outstretched to receive it. This could be related to the line of text above it saying that 'the Messiah fell & formed a heaven of what he stole from the Abyss', and that, according to the Gospel, 'he prays to the Father to send the comforter or Desire that Reason may have Ideas to build on.' By this interpretation Reason is leaving a long serpentine trail behind him. These lines are followed by a curious bent tree with two apples projecting from it,

ah fell. & formed a heaven of what he stole from the
Abyss

    This is shewn in the Gospel, where he prays to the
Father to send the comforter or Desire that Reason
may have Ideas to build on, the Jehovah of the Bible
being no other than **he**   who dwells in flaming fire.
Know that after Christs death, he became Jehovah.
    But in Milton; the Father is Destiny, the Son, a
Ratio of the five senses, & the Holy-ghost, Vacuum!
    Note. The reason Milton wrote in fetters when
he wrote of Angels & God, and at liberty when of
Devils & Hell, is because he was a true Poet and
of the Devils party without knowing it

A Memorable Fancy

    As I was walking among the fires of hell, de-
lighted with the enjoyments of Genius; which to An-
-gels look like torment and insanity. I collected some
of their Proverbs: thinking that as the sayings used
in a nation, mark its character, so the Proverbs of
Hell shew the nature of Infernal wisdom better
than any description of buildings or garments
    When I came home; on the abyss of the five sen-
-ses where a flat sided steep frowns over the pre-
-sent world. I saw a mighty Devil folded in black
clouds hovering on the sides of the rock, with cor

roding fires he wrote the following sentence now per-
ceved by the minds of men, & read by them on earth.

How do you know but ev'ry Bird that cuts the airy way,
Is an immense world of delight, clos'd by your senses five?

Proverbs of Hell

In seed time learn, in harvest teach, in winter enjoy.
Drive your cart and your plow over the bones of the dead.
The road of excess leads to the palace of wisdom.
Prudence is a rich ugly old maid courted by Incapacity.
He who desires but acts not, breeds pestilence.
The cut worm forgives the plow.
Dip him in the river who loves water.
A fool sees not the same tree that a wise man sees.
He whose face gives no light, shall never become a star
Eternity is in love with the productions of time.
The busy bee has no time for sorrow.
The hours of folly are measur'd by the clock, but of wis-
-dom: no clock can measure.
All wholsom food is caught without a net or a trap.
Bring out number weight & measure in a year of dearth
No bird soars too high, if he soars with his own wings.
A dead body, revenges not injuries.
The most sublime act is to set another before you.
If the fool would persist in his folly he would become
wise
Folly is the cloke of knavery.
Shame is Prides cloke.

perhaps indicating that he has fetched from the Abyss the fruit of the Tree of Knowledge.

In the sixth line Blake has made a change. The sentence as he first etched it was, 'the Jehovah of the Bible being no other than the Devil who dwells in flaming fire'. This Jehovah was for Blake an avenging Deity, whom he afterwards called Urizen, whereas his idea of a Christian God was one who, like Jesus, the artist and the source of energy, was willing to forgive all sins. The Devil, or Satan, had already been named a few lines above, and evidently Blake found it redundant to name him again, the description, 'he who dwells in flaming fire', being all that was needed. This error he could easily correct on his copperplate, or 'stereotype' as he sometimes called it, by removing the 't' of 'the' and the word 'Devil'. This left a gap, which he sometimes filled with a flame touched with gold.

In the middle of plate 6 is the heading 'A Memorable Fancy' for a passage which carries on into the first four lines of plate 7. To the sides of, and below, this heading the poet is seen joyously striding on flames and diving into them. The text relates how he was walking among the fires of Hell and collecting some of the Proverbs of Hell. As he came home he saw on an edge of 'the abyss of the five senses' 'a mighty Devil folded in black clouds', who (like Blake etching his copperplates) is writing in 'corroding fires' the following sentence:

How do you know but ev'ry Bird that cuts the airy way,
Is an immense world of delight, clos'd by your senses five?

These lines come at the top of plate 7, and among the black clouds billowing at the lower edge of plate 6 there is in most copies (though not in the one here reproduced), the letter H, acting as catchword for the third line on the next plate: 'How do you know but ev'ry Bird that cuts the airy way.' It appears that Blake derived the idea for these lines from Chatterton's 'The Dethe of Syr Charles Bawdin':

Howe dydd I knowe thatt ev'ry darte
Thatt cutte the airie waie
Myghte nott fynde passage toe my harte,
And close myne eyes for aie?

After the first four lines of plate 7 these four plates are occupied by the seventy proverbs which are the feature of the book found more attractive by most readers than any other, perhaps because they seem at first sight to be more easily understood.

It is recognized that these Proverbs were partly sparked off by the *Aphorisms* of Lavater, which were extensively annotated by Blake, often with approval, in his copy of the first edition of 1788. Johann Kaspar Lavater, Swiss moralist and friend of Henry Fuseli, was of the unpoetical school of Swedenborg and thus an Angel whose conventional and superficial thoughts were the very opposite of the imaginative and energetic attitudes of Blake's Devil. Foster Damon in his book on Blake's philosophy and symbols, 1924, has pointed out that Lavater wrote in Aphorism 466: 'An insult offered to a respectable character were often less pardonable than a precipitate murder', but that Blake went even beyond this in his Proverb: 'Sooner murder an Infant in its cradle than nurse unacted desires.' Damon commented that we cannot imagine Lavater either insulting a respectable character or committing precipitate murder, and while we should doubt Blake's capability of infanticide, yet this proverb would seem to classify 'unacted desires' as the greater crime. Blake indeed preached against all oppression, spiritual and physical, and voiced paradoxical exhortations to complete self-expression and contempt for the weak. 'He iterates', says Damon, 'the Truth of Imagination, the sanctity of every form of life, the wisdom of folly, and the danger of restraint'. A permissive society may tend to pluck Blake's Proverbs out of their satiric context and claim that they justify every kind of excess. Yet it must be remembered, as Damon says, that Blake praised excess, not for itself, but because it led to the palace of wisdom. 'Too much' is only second choice after 'Enough'.

The Proverbs of Hell are a distillation of satirical wisdom attained by experience and appreciation of the philosophical basis of Blake's Devil. They are best understood by being read in their proper context and then subjected to the reader's own meditation on their meaning. Individual 'explication' will only confuse and spoil their salty flavour.

There is only one major illustration placed at the foot of plate 10

Proverbs of Hell

Prisons are built with stones of Law, Brothels with bricks of Religion.

The pride of the peacock is the glory of God.

The lust of the goat is the bounty of God.

The wrath of the lion is the wisdom of God.

The nakedness of woman is the work of God.

Excess of sorrow laughs. Excess of joy weeps.

The roaring of lions, the howling of wolves, the raging of the stormy sea, and the destructive sword, are portions of eternity too great for the eye of man.

The fox condemns the trap, not himself.

Joys impregnate, Sorrows bring forth.

Let man wear the fell of the lion, woman the fleece of the sheep.

The bird a nest, the spider a web, man friendship.

The selfish smiling fool, & the sullen frowning fool, shall be both thought wise, that they may be a rod.

What is now proved was once, only imagin'd.

The rat, the mouse, the fox, the rabbet; watch the roots, the lion, the tyger, the horse, the elephant, watch the fruits.

The cistern contains: the fountain overflows

One thought, fills immensity.

Always be ready to speak your mind, and a base man will avoid you.

Every thing possible to be believ'd is an image of truth.

The eagle never lost so much time, as when he submit--ted to learn of the crow.

The

9

Proverbs of Hell

The fox provides for himself, but God provides for the lion

Think in the morning. Act in the noon, Eat in the evening, Sleep in the night.

He who has sufferd you to impose on him knows you.

As the plow follows words, so God rewards prayers.

The tygers of wrath are wiser than the horses of instruction

Expect poison from the standing water.

You never know what is enough unless you know what is more than enough.

Listen to the fools reproach! it is a kingly title!

The eyes of fire, the nostrils of air, the mouth of water, the beard of earth.

The weak in courage is strong in cunning.

The apple tree never asks the beech how he shall grow nor the lion, the horse; how he shall take his prey.

The thankful reciever bears a plentiful harvest

If others had not been foolish, we should be so.

The soul of sweet delight, can never be defil'd,

When thou seest an Eagle, thou seest a portion of Genius. lift up thy head!

As the catterpiller chooses the fairest leaves to lay her eggs on, so the priest lays his curse on the fairest joys.

To create a little flower is the labour of ages.

Damn, braces: Bless relaxes.

The best wine is the oldest, the best water the newest

Prayers plow not! Praises reap not!

Joys laugh not! Sorrows weep not!

beneath the exclamation : 'Enough! or Too much'. The scene shews three figures at the foaming edge of the Sea of Time and Space. In the centre the Devil is kneeling with a scroll lying across his knees and presumably carrying the Proverbs. He is pointing impatiently to the first lines to instruct a slow-witted Angel industriously writing them down in a book on his knees, while probably misunderstanding them. Behind the Devil is a kind of throne or judgement seat from which he seems to have descended in his impatience. Sprouting from his back are spiky wings, their points directed respectively to the words 'Enough' and 'Too much'. To his left and behind him is seated a contrasted figure, alert and interested, with his own script nearly finished across his knees while he leans over to see how the stupid Angel is progressing. Erdman suggests that this is 'an apprentice Devil', perhaps Blake himself. A very noticeable detail is the spiky plant (not well defined in this copy) curling beside the stupid Angel; this was plainly taken, as noted by Erdman, from the plate facing page 15 in Erasmus Darwin's *Loves of the Plants* (Part II of *The Botanic Garden*), 1789, illustrating the spiked leaves of the Catch-fly plant or sundew *(Dionaea muscipula)*, which folds up to catch and destroy any insect attempting to reach the seed. The Angel sitting between this predatory plant and the spiky wings of his instructor is fairly caught. By contrast the clever fellow on the other side is flanked by fine free growths resembling that of *Gloriosa superba*, a flower illustrated on the previous plate in Darwin's book, facing page 14. The design seems to imply that the stupid Angel must receive and understand the Devil's Proverbs if he is to be saved.

There are numerous interlinear decorations on all the plates in this section:

Plate 7: To the left of the title is a stooping figure dibbling with a stick in the ground—'In seed time learn'. To the right is a talking serpent giving the joyful message—'in harvest teach, in winter enjoy'—

to a woman and two children, who receive it with arms raised in pleasure. Six lines lower down is a running man with hands raised as if making an announcement. Behind him are vague plants touched with gold and perhaps he is carrying the general message of joy. At the foot of the page is a trumpeter with trailing gown floating in a blue sky. It seems that all the small decorations are helping to proclaim the good news conveyed by the Proverbs that 'Energy is eternal Delight'.

Plate 8: The decorations suggest in a general way fertility and hope—a bunch of grapes, flowers, soaring or singing birds. In the middle of the page a proverb is directly illustrated by a strip shewing two people on their knees fashioning garments from 'the fell of the lion . . . the fleece of the sheep', with a lion and a grazing sheep on either side.

Four lines lower down a foolish man, personifying 'the rat, the mouse, the fox, the rabbet' of the text, watches the roots of a barren tree. Two lines below this is a seascape with ships and birds; a cliff projects into the sea on the right with a tree growing from its edge.

Below this is a confrontation between a serpent and a galloping stag apparently illustrating the proverb:

Always be ready to speak your mind, and a base man will avoid you.

Erdman suggests that Blake is drawing on the tradition that the serpent and the stag are natural enemies.

Proverbs of Hell

The head Sublime, the heart Pathos, the genitals Beauty
the hands & feet Proportion.

As the air to a bird or the sea to a fish, so is contempt
to the contemptible.

The crow wishd every thing was black, the owl, that eve-
ry thing was white.

Exuberance is Beauty.

If the lion was advised by the fox, he would be cunning.

Improvent makes strait roads, but the crooked roads
without Improvement, are roads of Genius.

Sooner murder an Infant in its cradle than nurse unact-
ed desires

Where man is not nature is barren.

Truth can never be told so as to be understood, and
not be believd.

Enough! or Too.much

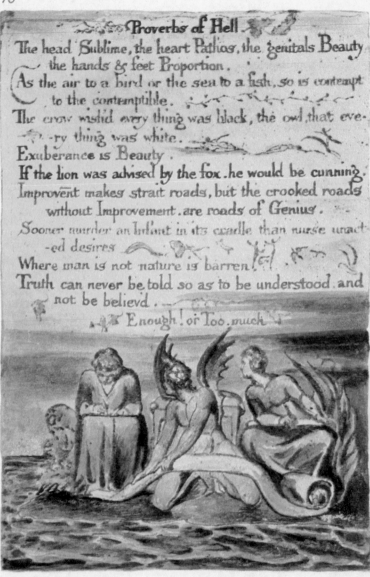

The ancient Poets animated all sensible objects
with Gods or Geniuses, calling them by the names and
adorning them with the properties of woods, rivers
mountains, lakes, cities, nations, and whatever their
enlarged & numerous senses could perceive.

And particularly they studied the genius of each
city & country, placing it under its mental deity.

Till a system was formed, which some took ad
vantage of & enslav'd the vulgar by attempting to
realize or abstract the mental deities from their
objects: thus began Priesthood.

Choosing forms of worship from poetic tales.

And at length they pronounced that the Gods
had orderd such things.

Thus men forgot that All deities reside
in the human breast.

Plates 7-10 (cont.)

Plate 9 : The decorations are mostly vague patches of colour, until at the foot of the page a couple (body and soul) are flying out of the right-hand corner as if to encourage the reader to proceed.

Plate 10 : The decorations formed by strips of figures flying or dancing in exuberant attitudes seem to illustrate the central line of the page, 'Exuberance is Beauty', though one figure remains lying

apparently not yet aware of the general exuberance around him. Below is the design already described.

Plate 11

The text of this plate is concerned with the origin of anthropomorphic religions as conceived by the Ancient Poets, who endowed natural objects and places with the names and properties of Gods or Geniuses. The systems thus invented led to the formation of a Priesthood, the priests then announcing that the Gods had so ordained them. The divinity of Man himself was forgotten.

The illustration at the head of the page shews Nature appearing in its spiritual forms. On the left a Sun-god is arising from the ground. In front, a stream in the form of a nude woman is tending a flower springing up as a child. Behind this group is a tree trunk with the face of an old man appearing on its bark.

At the foot of the page is Blake's Urizen, maker of the material world, creating Man in a design reminiscent of Michelangelo's painting in the Vatican of God creating Adam. Here the newly created Man is drifting away into dark clouds, his divinity forgotten.

The interlinear decorations are few. Among the first four lines are a number of soaring birds. Lower down, after the word 'Priesthood', is a wavy hieroglyph reminding us that a serpent was not infrequently Blake's symbol for the priest of organized religion. Following the last line but two is a priest exhorting four worshippers on their knees before the headless figure of Power carrying a sword.

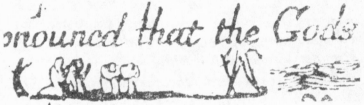

12

A Memorable Fancy.

The Prophets Isaiah and Ezekiel dined with me, and I asked them how they dared so roundly to assert. that God spoke to them; and whether they did not think at the time, that they would be misunderstood, & so be the cause of imposition

Isaiah answer'd. I saw no God. nor heard any. in a finite organical perception: but my senses discover'd the infinite in every thing, and as I was then perswaded. & remain confirm'd; that the voice of honest indignation is the voice of God. I cared not for consequences but wrote

Then I asked: does a firm perswasion that a thing is so, make it so?

He replied. All poets believe that it does. & in ages of imagination this firm perswasion removed mountains; but many are not capable of a firm perswasion of any thing

Then Ezekiel said. The philosophy of the east taught the first principles of human perception some nations held one principle for the origin & some another, we of Israel taught that the Poetic Genius (as you now call it) was the first principle and all the others merely derivative. which was the cause of our despising the Priests & Philosophers of other countries. and prophecying that all Gods

would

would at last be proved to originate in ours & to be the tributaries of the Poetic Genius, it was this that our great poet King David desired so fervently & invokes so patheticly, saying by this he conquers enemies & governs kingdoms; and we so loved our God, that we cursed in his name all the deities of surrounding nations, and asserted that they had rebelled; from these opinions the vulgar came to think that all nations would at last be subject to the jews.

This said he, like all firm perswasions, is come to pass, for all nations believe the jews code and worship the jews god, and what greater subjection can be

I heard this with some wonder, & must confess my own conviction. After dinner I askd Isaiah to favour the world with his last works, he said none of equal value was lost. Ezekiel said the same of his.

I also asked Isaiah what made him go naked and barefoot three years? he answerd, the same that made our friend Diogenes the Grecian.

I then asked Ezekiel. why he eat dung, & lay so long on his right & left side? he answerd, the desire of raising other men into a perception of the infinite this the North American tribes practise. & is he honest who resists his genius or conscience, only for the sake of present ease or gratification?

These plates relate the second 'Memorable Fancy', beginning with
the surprising words, 'The Prophets Isaiah and Ezekiel dined with
me'. Contemporary and later critics have seized on this statement as
indubitable evidence of Blake's insanity, ignoring the implication
of the heading that the story is a 'Fancy', an experience of the imag-
ination. Blake used the discussion with the two prophets to hammer
in the poet's conviction that the imagination is more revealing of the
truth than any 'finite organical perception', that is, the limiting
cavern of man's five senses. He asks questions in order that the
prophets may confirm his beliefs by their answers. The question
'does a firm perswasion that a thing is so, make it so?', is thus seen to
be a statement of the truth. Poetic Genius is the first principle and
perceives 'the infinite in every thing'. The references to Isaiah's
going barefoot and Ezekiel's eating dung and laying so long on his
right and left sides are to justify the exhibition of any eccentricity
in order to draw attention to poetic truths.

There are no major illustrations to this philosophic discussion with
Blake's imaginary guests, and the interlinear decorations are for the
most part indeterminate vegetable and serpentine forms or flying
figures of men or birds giving emphasis to various words or passages.
The final detail at the foot of plate 13 is more definitely related to the
text. The Prophet Ezekiel is seen laying on his right side, the length
of his rippling bed expressing the long duration of his self-imposed
ordeal.

Plate 14

In this brief passage Blake uses the ancient tradition that 'the world will be consumed in fire at the end of six thousand years', perhaps relating it to the French and American revolutions. The cherub with the flaming sword, the guardian, that is, of the world of restriction, has been commanded to leave the Tree of Life, lost when Adam was driven from Paradise. Man again has access to the Tree and everything is transformed from the limitations of materialism to a state of infiniteness and holiness. This is accomplished by a general widening of the senses, especially of sexual enjoyment. Blake again refers to this uncovering of the identity of the soul and the body by means of the corrosive fluids used in making his books, thus releasing man from the cavern of his ordinary senses.

The illustration at the top of the page shews a woman with outstretched arms against a background of flames, hovering over the greyish sleeping body of a man. This symbolizes the resuscitation of the caverned man by the female soul with the flaming energy of increased desires.

In the middle of the page 'sensual enjoyment' is followed by living oak leaves and burrs, and in the next line a leaf hangs from 'body'. Near the foot of the page is a prancing horse expressing energy released.

The ancient tradition that the world will be con--sumed in fire at the end of six thousand years is true, as I have heard from Hell.

For the cherub with his flaming sword is hereby commanded to leave his guard at tree of life, and when he does, the whole creation will be consumed, and appear infinite. and holy whereas it now appears finite & corrupt.

This will come to pass by an improvement of sensual enjoyment.

But first the notion that man has a body distinct from his soul, is to be expunged; this I shall do by printing in the infernal method, by corrosives, which in Hell are salutary and me-dicinal, melting apparent surfaces away, and displaying the infinite which was hid.

If the doors of perception were cleansed every thing would appear to man as it is: In-finite

For man has closed himself up, till he sees all things thro' narrow chinks of his cavern.

15

A Memorable Fancy

I was in a Printing house in Hell & saw the method in which knowledge is transmitted from generation to generation

In the first chamber was a Dragon-Man, clearing away the rubbish from a caves mouth; within, a number of Dragons were hollowing the cave.

In the second chamber was a Viper folding round the rock & the cave, and others adorning it with gold silver and precious stones

In the third chamber was an Eagle with wings and feathers of air, he caused the inside of the cave to be infinite, around were numbers of Eagle like men, who built palaces in the immense cliffs.

In the fourth chamber were Lions of flaming fire raging around & melting the metals into living fluids.

In the fifth chamber were Unnam'd forms, which cast the metals into the expanse. There they were reciev'd by Men who occupied the sixth chamber, and took the forms of books & were arranged in libraries.

Plate 15 A MEMORABLE FANCY

This plate carries the third 'Memorable Fancy' giving a fantastic allegory of how knowledge is transmitted from generation to generation. Blake places himself 'in a Printing house in Hell' and describes six chambers or caves symbolizing, as always, the caverned man, limited by his five senses.

The first chamber contains a 'Dragon-Man', symbol of sensual pleasure, clearing away the rubbish of conventional laws and thereby liberating man for the better development of his imagination.

In the second chamber the Viper of Reason is helping the expansion of knowledge with gold and silver decorations (such as Blake might have used in his illuminations of his pages) and thus also the improvement of spiritual perception.

In the third chamber the improvements have enabled the Eagle of Genius to build palaces for Man's creative faculties. In the fourth and fifth chambers Blake saw the actual process of melting and casting metals for the making of books, suggesting his own use of copper-plates as well as the casting of types. In the sixth chamber the resulting books were being taken in charge by librarians.

The illustration below the text shews the Eagle of Genius carrying up the Viper of Reason, the two thus co-operating in the progressive improvement of perception.

The smaller decorations are few. At the top the usual figures of Body and Soul on either side of the heading are both attached by threads to the letters. Most of the third line is occupied by a convoluted string expressing the continuous unfolding of knowledge, ending, according to Erdman, 'ironically with a Shandean delete sign', referring to the looped flourish represented by the movement of Corporal Trim's stick in *Tristram Shandy*, 1782, vol. VI, chap. xxiv. The leaves at the end of the sixth line and elsewhere suggest the leaves of a book. At the close of the ninth line a sinuous stroke, the Viper of Reason perhaps, leads to two figures, standing and reclining with a book on the ground between them.

Plate 16 and upper part of Plate 17

The illustration at the top of plate 16 has a superficial resemblance to Blake's engraving in his small emblem book of about the same period, *The Gates of Paradise* (plate 12), shewing Count Ugolino with his sons and grandsons dying in prison (a subject fron Dante's *Divine Comedy*), but the group on this plate has a different meaning. It illustrates the first lines of the text describing 'The Giants who formed this world', that is, the five senses of Man, the source of our Energies. These Giants live in chains, controlled by the cunning, weak intelligences of the Reasoners. Blake then divides mankind into two categories of 'Prolific', or imaginative and creative minds, and 'Devourers', or Reasoners, who take 'portions of existence' and fancy them to be the whole. He explains that the Prolific is not to be identified with God. He is the creative Man through whom God is manifested. This Blake expressed very plainly in his later poem, 'The Everlasting Gospel', in the lines:

> Thou art a Man, God is no more,
> Thine own Humanity learn to Adore

In the concluding sentences on plate 17 Blake explains further that the two kinds of men are natural enemies, whom religion tries to reconcile, though Christ did not do this, separating them into the sheep and goats of his parable. Finally it is explained that Satan, or the Tempter, was formerly thought to be one of the antediluvian Giants of Genesis, 6:4, who are our Energies.

The first interlinear decoration on plate 16 is a little figure with outstretched arms standing near the end of a long wavy line, perhaps

a Devourer, happily imagining that his end of the line is All. Three lines lower is vegetation, the excess of the Devourers' delights.

16

The Giants who formed this world into its
sensual existence and now seem to live in it
in chains; are in truth, the causes of its life
& the sources of all activity, but the chains
are, the cunning of weak and tame minds, which
have power to resist energy. according to the pro-
verb, the weak in courage is strong in cunning

Thus one portion of being, is the Prolific, the
other, the Devouring: to the devourer it seems as
if the producer was in his chains, but it is not so,
he only takes portions of existence and fancies
that the whole. —

But the Prolific would cease to be Prolific
unless the Devourer as a sea recieved the excess
of his delights. —

Some will say, Is not God alone the Prolific
I answer, God only Acts & Is, in existing beings
or Men. —

These two classes of men are always upon
earth, & they should be enemies; whoever tries
to

to reconcile them seeks to destroy existence.

Religion is an endeavour to reconcile the two.

Note. Jesus Christ did not wish to unite but to seperate them, as in the Parable of sheep and goats! & he says I came not to send Peace but a Sword.

Messiah or Satan or Tempter was formerly thought to be one of the Antediluvians who are our Energies.

A Memorable Fancy

An Angel came to me and said. O pitiable foolish young man! O horrible! O dreadful state! consider the hot burning dungeon thou art preparing for thyself to all eternity, to which thou art going in such career.

I said. perhaps you will be willing to shew me my eternal lot & we will contemplate together upon it and see whether your lot or mine is most desirable

So he took me thro' a stable & thro' a church & down into the church vault at the end of which was a mill: thro' the mill we went, and came to a cave. down the winding cavern we groped our tedi-ous way till a void boundless as a nether sky ap-peard beneath us & we held by the roots of trees and hung over this immensity; but I said, if you please we will commit ourselves to this void, and see whether providence is here also, if you will not I will? but he answerd, do not presume O young-man but as we here remain behold thy lot which will soon appear when the darkness passes away

So I remaind with him sitting in the twisted

Three lines below, most of the space is occupied by a vision of the Body and Soul striving to form a Man by reaching towards one another over vegetable objects.

At the top of plate 17 in the right-hand corner is a pine tree with branches pointing to the first two lines. In the sixth line is a series of emblems—a sheep grazing and a goat standing on its hind legs, a static horse and a galloping horse—each pair symbolizing the Devourer

and the Prolific. The galloping horse will recur in a more splendid form on the last plate.

Plates 17-20   A MEMORABLE FANCY

These four plates relate the longest of the 'Memorable Fancies', in which Blake carries on a fantastic, almost comic, argument with a pompous Swedenborgian Angel, mouthpiece of conventional religion. The Angel warns him of his dreadful fate if he continues to pursue his chosen course. Blake replies by suggesting that the Angel exhibit to him his (Blake's) 'eternal lot' and that they then contemplate whether his or the Angel's lot is the more desirable. They accordingly descend into an abstract world described in concrete terms of great satirical power, both visually effective and humourously absurd.

The stages of their descent and the objects they see need some explanation for proper appreciation of the satire. The stable shelters the tame 'horses of instruction'; the church is the house of orthodox religion, leading to a vault, the tomb of dead passions; the mill is the home of sterile materialistic reasoning where the Angel resides; the cave is the dwelling of 'the caverned man', already a familiar figure. The explorers then reach the Abyss, a Swedenborgian conception of Heaven and Hell, in which every conventional individual has his predestinated place. Blake hangs over the void, supported by the roots of trees, that is, the principle of vegetative or material existence, and comes to rest in 'the twisted root of an oak'—the sacred tree of the Druids and therefore emblem of ancient error (Blake was there on false pretences). The Angel hangs on an inverted fungus representing some blind dogma, which gives him satisfaction. Together they hang over the Abyss and watch what is happening by the strange light of a sun, which is 'black but shining', that is, according to Damon, an orb providing the heat of Wrath, but none of the light of Truth. Here the spirits of Blake and his like are tormented by monstrous shapes of black and white (that is, good and evil) spiders, or Powers of the air, contending for their souls, recalling the things seen in old pictures of the Last Judgement. The Angel tells Blake that his place is between the black and white spiders, the place of greatest torment. Presently they see something approaching from the East, the realm of the emotions in Blake's divisions of the compass, being also the region where Christ was born and died. It is the head of the great Leviathan, a symbol presumably derived from the *Leviathan* of Thomas Hobbes. To Blake the monster is the Serpent of Materialism as conceived by Hobbes in his account of the State, or Commonwealth, governed by a crowned king and the power of organized religion. This Leviathan, advancing through the Sea of Time and Space, is described as having his forehead 'divided into streaks of green & purple like those on a tyger's forehead', which corresponds with the colouring seen in some illustrations of 'The Tyger' in the later book, *Songs of Experience*.

The Angel is so horrified by what he sees that he climbs back into his mill, whereupon Blake finds himself sitting alone on a pleasant bank, listening happily to a harper who sings of the man who never changes his opinion, thereby breeding reptiles of the mind. This renewed and rejuvenated man is illustrated on plate 21.

On rejoining the Angel in the mill, Blake explains that he escaped unharmed because the whole scene was an illusion produced by the Angel's conventional ideas. He then offers to shew the Angel his lot in the Blakean conception of Eternity. Seizing the unwilling Angel in his arms and flying westward he plunges into the body of the sun, that is, mental illumination, taking with him Swedenborg's books, called by Damon 'the Baedekers of the spiritual world'. They then

root of an oak, he was suspended in a fungus
which hung with the head downward into the deep;

By degrees we beheld the infinite Abyss, fiery
as the smoke of a burning city, beneath us at an
immense distance was the sun, black but shining
round it were fiery tracks on which revolv'd vast
spiders, crawling after their prey; which flew or
rather swum in the infinite deep, in the most ter-
-rific shapes of animals sprung from corruption.
& the air was full of them, & seemd composed
of them; these are Devils, and are called Powers
of the air, I now asked my companion which was my
eternal lot? he said, between the black & white spiders

But now, from between the black & white spiders
a cloud and fire burst and rolled thro the deep
blackning all beneath, so that the nether deep grew
black as a sea & rolled with a terrible noise: be-
-neath us was nothing now to be seen but a black
tempest, till looking east between the clouds & the
waves, we saw a cataract of blood mixed with fire
and not many stones throw from us appeard and
sunk again the scaly fold of a monstrous serpent.
at last to the east, distant about three degrees ap-
peard a fiery crest above the waves slowly it rear-
ed like a ridge of golden rocks till we discoverd
two globes of crimson fire, from which the sea
fled away in clouds of smoke, and now we saw, it
was the head of **Leviathan**. his forehead was di-
vided into streaks of green & purple like those on
a tygers forehead; soon we saw his mouth & red
gills hang just above the raging foam tinging the
black deep with beams of blood, advancing toward
us

us with all the fury of a spiritual existence.

My friend the Angel climb'd up from his station into the mill; I remain'd alone. & then this appearance was no more, but I found myself sitting on a pleasant bank beside a river by moon light hearing a harper who sung to the harp. & his theme was, The man who never alters his opinion is like standing water, & breeds reptiles of the mind.

But I arose, and sought for the mill & there I found my Angel, who surprised asked me, how I escaped?

I answer'd. All that we saw was owing to your metaphysics: for when you ran away, I found myself on a bank by moonlight hearing a harper, But now we have seen my eternal lot, shall I shew you yours? he laugh'd at my proposal: but I by force suddenly caught him in my arms, & flew westerly thro' the night, till we were elevated above the earths shadow: then I flung myself with him directly into the body of the sun, here I clothed myself in white, & taking in my hand Swedenborgs volumes sunk from the glorious clime, and passed all the planets till we came to saturn, here I staid to rest & then leap'd into the void, between saturn & the fixed stars.

Here said I! is your lot, in this space, if space it may be call'd, Soon we saw the stable and the church, & I took him to the altar and open'd the Bible, and lo! it was a deep pit, into which I descended driving the Angel before me, soon we saw seven houses of brick, one we enter'd; in it were a
num

leap into the void between the planets and find themselves again entering the stables and the church already described. Blake opens the Bible which he finds lying on the altar and it proves to be the entrance to the pit of established religion with its seven chambers, or Churches, where the Devourers in simian shapes, representing the various religions, are preying on one another, though chained by their middles like performing monkeys. Blake and the Angel are overcome by the stench of this internecine conflict and retreat again into the mill, Blake taking with him the skeleton of one body. This turns out to be nothing but 'Aristotle's Analytics', that is, the logic of materialism, and the Angel is dismissed as a time-wasting metaphysician.

The 'Fancy' ends with an imposing visual image of the coiled Leviathan rolling in the Sea of Time and Space. Below this is the aphorism, partly obliterated by paint in some copies of the book (as in this one):

Opposition is true Friendship

another paradoxical 'Proverb of Hell' embodying much truth.

The heading of the fourth 'Memorable Fancy' on plate 17 is flanked on the left by a drooping tree from which the large reddish-coloured bird in the centre has just taken flight. This is the Phoenix of resurgent imagination. Standing with his back to the tree is a man, a Reasoner, gazing out over an empty land devoid of interest. On the right is the recurrent group of five birds arising from the ground to represent the five senses stimulated to activity by the Phoenix.

Plate 18 has no interlinear decorations. On plate 19 there are decorations in three spaces. Firstly, following the words 'reptiles of the mind', are the figures of body and soul streaking parallel with one another towards a cloud, beyond which there are two soaring birds.

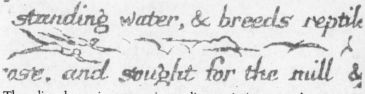

Three lines lower is a serpentine curlicue pointing towards two more birds, and the next line begins with a tiny running man (only dimly seen in this copy), perhaps the escaping Angel. Seven lines from the foot of the page are again the body and soul meeting in the air to

touch hands. Beyond this is another bird and the dragon form with serpentine body already seen on plate 5.

Near the end of plate 20 on the right-hand side are three simian shapes illustrating the inhabitants of the seven Churches. Above the

vision of Leviathan, in the right-hand margin, Blake can be seen sitting in the roots of a tree, though in this copy he is almost lost in the clouds billowing over the apparition.

number of monkeys, baboons, & all of that species
chaind by the middle, grinning and snatching at
one another. but witheld by the shortness of their
chains; however I saw that they sometimes grew nu
merous, and then the weak were caught by the strong
and with a grinning aspect, first coupled with & then
devourd, by plucking off first one limb and then ano-
ther till the body was left a helpless trunk. this after
grinning & kissing it with seeming fondness they de-
vourd too; and here & there I saw one savourily pic-
king the flesh off of his own tail; as the stench ter-
ribly annoyd us both we went into the mill, & I in
my hand brought the skeleton of a body, which in
the mill was Aristotles Analytics.

So the Angel said: thy phantasy has imposed
upon me & thou oughtest to be ashamed.

I answerd: we impose on one another. & it is
but lost time to converse with you whose works
are only Analytics

I have always found that Angels have the vani-
-ty to speak of themselves as the only wise; this they
do with a confident insolence spiriting from systema-
-tic reasoning:

Thus Swedenborg boasts that what he writes is
new; tho' it is only the Contents or Index of already
publish'd books

A man carried a monkey about for a shew, & be-
-cause he was a little wiser than the monkey, grew
vain, and concievd himself as much wiser than se-
-ven men. It is so with Swedenborg; he shews the
folly of churches & exposes hypocrites, till he im
agines that all are religious, & himself the single
                                                    one

Plate 21 and upper part of Plate 22

The text of these plates shews Blake pausing in his flow of 'Memorable Fancies' to devote a passage to general criticism of Swedenborg and his works, taking him as the type of self-satisfied Angel resting on the results of systematic Reasoning, largely derived from other writers.

The illustration at the top of plate 21 refers back to the passage on plate 19, where Blake, escaped from the horrors of Swedenborg's idea of Eternity, finds himself 'sitting on a pleasant bank beside a river'. He feels happy and renewed after having disposed of the Angel's falsities, and he is seated (in this copy of the book) among rays of light beginning to penetrate the dispersing clouds of error. His left knee rests negligently on a human skull, perhaps recalling the Proverb of Hell, 'Drive your cart and your plow over the bones of the dead', or more probably, the discarded skeleton at the end of the 'Memorable Fancy', 'which in the mill was Aristotle's Analytics'. Blake used the emblem of the 'Regenerated Man' on more than one occasion in other contexts (*America*, plate 6, 1793; 'Death's Door' in his illustrations to Blair's *Grave*, 1808).

The small decorations above the first line of text are all related, as Erdman notes, to education. At the left-hand end a woman with little wings of intellect is seated on the stalk of a ripe ear of corn and receives a small child with her hands; after several loops a larger

child is studying a book on the ground with the help of an adult on the other side of the book; at the end of the line a boy is seated reading

alone in his book, like the reader at the top of the tree in the decoration of 'The School-Boy' in *Songs of Innocence*. Other spaces are filled with looping lines and vegetable forms.

On plate 22 the first line ends with a contorted design which Erdman sees as a large fish twisting wildly in a long net, the end

being held by a fisherman seated on a slope at the right. Three lines lower down a human figure entangled in a leafy branch points to the

words, 'And now hear the reason'. Four lines below is a broken row of loops illustrating Swedenborg's inability to converse with Devils, and in the next break Swedenborg's 'superficial opinions' are indicated by flat leaves without character. Near the centre of the plate the ideas to be derived from Dante or Shakespeare are illustrated by an assemblage of birds and insects.

Plates 22-24   A MEMORABLE FANCY

The lower part of plate 22 and the next two carry the fifth and last 'Memorable Fancy', telling of 'a Devil in a flame of fire' (that is, Blake himself), who chose to shock an Angel by stating that 'The worship of God is Honouring his gifts in other men', thus identifying God with Man. The Angel, after several colour changes like a chameleon's, recovers from the shock and rebukes him as an idolator, naming Christ only as One with God and as the visible law-giver, all other men being nothing. The Devil counters with the statement that Christ himself, by acting upon impulse, broke all the Commandments, though he was the greatest and most virtuous of men. This was elaborated in Blake's later poem 'The Everlasting Gospel'.

22

one on earth that ever broke a net.

Now hear a plain fact: Swedenborg has not written one new truth: Now hear another: he has written all the old falshoods.

And now hear the reason. He conversed with Angels who are all religious. & conversed not with Devils who all hate religion for he was incapable thro' his conceited notions.

Thus Swedenborgs writings are a recapitulation of all superficial opinions, and an analysis of the more sublime. but no further.

Have now another plain fact: Any man of mechanical talents may from the writings of Paracelsus or Jacob Behmen, produce ten thousand volumes of equal value with Swedenborgs, and from those of Dante or Shakespear, an infinite number.

But when he has done this, let him not say that he knows better than his master, for he only holds a candle in sunshine.

A Memorable Fancy

Once I saw a Devil in a flame of fire, who arose before an Angel that sat on a cloud. and the Devil utterd these words.

The worship of God is. Honouring his gifts in other men each according to his genius. and loving the great

greatest men best, those who envy or calumniate
great men hate God, for there is no other God.

The Angel hearing this became almost blue
but mastering himself he grew yellow, & at last
white pink & smiling. and then replied,

Thou Idolater. is not God One? & is not he
visible in Jesus Christ? and has not Jesus Christ
given his sanction to the law of ten commandments
and are not all other men fools sinners & nothings?

The Devil answer'd; bray a fool in a morter with
wheat yet shall not his folly be beaten out of him
if Jesus Christ is the greatest man, you ought to
love him in the greatest degree; now hear how he
has given his sanction to the law of ten command
ments; did he not mock at the sabbath, and so
mock the sabbaths God? murder those who were
murderd because of him? turn away the law from
the woman taken in adultery? steal the labor of
others to support him? bear false witness when
he omitted making a defence before Pilate? covet
when he pray'd for his disciples, and when he bid
them shake off the dust of their feet against such
as refused to lodge them? I tell you, no virtue
can exist without breaking these ten command-
ments; Jesus was all virtue, and acted from im-
-pulse

In a 'Note' Blake tells how the Angel has now become his friend and a Devil, with whom he often reads the Bible in 'its infernal or diabolical sense', concluding with the promise that he has also 'The Bible of Hell: which the world shall have whether they will or no'. It is conjectured that this promise may refer to the later Illuminated Books in which Blake developed his philosophy and his prophecies.

Plate 24 finishes up with a final proverb against the tyranny of Law engraved below an illustration depicting Nebuchadnezzar, the type of man debased and brutalized until he tries to live by eating grass, that is, the mental food provided by the world of materialism. He is crawling on hands and knees with an expression of terror on his face. Blake afterwards developed this horrific image in one of his large monotypes made in 1793-4.

The small decorations surrounding the heading of this 'Memorable Fancy' on plate 22 are difficult to relate to the text. On the left is a figure reclining in a curve, like Ezekiel, on his right side, though facing the spectator. Above is a flying figure apparently pursuing a serpent and almost catching its tail in his hand. To the right of this

is a figure apparently transfixed by an arrow from a leaping archer's bow, perhaps the Angel receiving the shock of the Devil's words.

In the third line are flowers and various vegetable forms. Below the last line is a kind of vegetable serpent over grey water.

At the foot of plate 23 is a series of strange forms, beginning on the left with the Serpent of Reason shewing a wide gaping mouth,

ready to devour all those unable to defy the commandments which are listed in the text as those broken by Jesus Christ. These are shewn as an animal on its back, legs in air, two human figures in a state of collapse, and a nondescript worm. These are followed

in the first line of plate 24 by a thinker huddled in doubt about the preceding questions. Further to the right he breaks free in the form of the Angel 'embracing the flame of fire'. Below the fourth line is

a group of six people engaged in reading books, presumably Blake's Bible of Hell, with a pile of discarded volumes behind them.

pulse: not from rules.

When he had so spoken: I beheld the Angel who
stretched out his arms embracing the flame of fire
& he was consumed and arose as Elijah.

Note. This Angel, who is now become a Devil, is
my particular friend: we often read the Bible to-
gether in its infernal or diabolical sense which
the world shall have if they behave well.

I have also: The Bible of Hell: which the world
shall have whether they will or no.

One Law for the Lion & Ox is Oppression

25

A Song of Liberty

1. The Eternal Female groand! it was heard over all the Earth.

2. Albions coast is sick, silent; the American meadows faint!

3 Shadows of Prophecy shiver along by the lakes and the rivers and mutter acrofs the ocean! France rend down thy dungeon;

4. Golden Spain burst the barriers of old Rome;

5. Cast thy keys O Rome into the deep down falling, even to eternity down falling,

6 And weep!

7. In her trembling hands she took the new born terror howling;

8. On those infinite mountains of light now barr'd out by the atlantic sea, the new born fire stood before the starry king!

9. Flag'd with grey brow'd snows and thunderous visages the jealous wings wav'd over the deep.

10. The speary hand burned aloft, unbuckled was the shield, forth went the hand of jealousy among the flaming hair, and

All copies of *The Marriage of Heaven and Hell* end with these three plates carrying 'A Song of Liberty', forming, in twenty numbered sentences an apocalyptic finale to the central theme of the book—the superiority of the creative views of a rebellious Devil to those of a conventional and conservative Angel. This doctrine had in 1790 found its justification in the French and American revolutions. In apocalyptic language Blake welcomed these events, which he thought would lead to the liberation of mankind from tyranny (in the shape of King George) over thought and action, and from repression by the priests of organized religion, personified in the Church of Rome, whose overthrow is specifically celebrated in the 'Chorus' at the end.

In the sixteenth sentence of the 'Song' Blake added to the Rintrah of 'The Argument' one more of his personifications of abstract ideas by the name 'Urthona'. This is one of the 'Four Zoas' of Blake's conception of Man's nature: Tharmas, his body; Urizen, his reason; Luvah, his emotions; and Urthona, his imagination. All of these were explained only in later writings, yet Blake was content to throw in one of these Zoas, unexplained, among the consequences of Revolution, perhaps because it must have been to him the most important result of all. Urthona concerned Art and the Divinity of Man and worked darkly in the 'dens' of the subconscious mind, but would be liberated by the collapse of Tyranny.

In the eighteenth sentence Tyranny is still leading his 'starry hosts' ('starry' because stars always symbolized for Blake the Newtonian universe, limiting man's perception) and promulgating his ten commands. But 'the son of fire', that is, Orc, the spirit of Revolt, is victorious in the golden dawn, stamping 'the stony law to dust, loosing the eternal horses from the dens of night', and proclaiming the climactic sentence:

Empire is no more! and now the lion & wolf shall cease.

The plates of 'A Song of Liberty' have no major illustrations. The interlinear decorations on plate 25 are for the most part flowering plants and soaring birds, emblems of energetic life. At the end of the seventh sentence 'The Eternal Female' of the first sentence is shewn taking 'the new born terror', as green flames, in her hands.

On plate 26 in the second line the menacing stag, first seen on

plate 8, seems to represent the tyrant king dashing towards the diving figure of 'the new born terror', or Orc. In the eighth line are two

seated figures perhaps representing the Jew counting gold and the African. After the sixteenth sentence a floating figure appears to summon Urthona, seated in his den, to freedom. In the third line

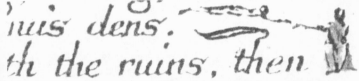

from the foot of the page is 'the gloomy king' stretching his arms towards two pairs of counsellors.

On plate 27 in the third line is a warrior fallen on one knee in vain pursuit of 'the son of fire', who, in the sixth line, has loosed 'the

26

hurl'd the new born wonder thro' the starry
night

11. The fire, the fire, is falling!

12. Look up! look up! O citizen of London
enlarge thy countenance; O Jew, leave coun
-ting gold, return to thy oil and wine: O
African! black African! (go. winged thought
widen his forehead.)

13. The fiery limbs, the flaming hair, shot
like the sinking sun into the western sea.

14. Wak'd from his eternal sleep, the hoary
element roaring fled away:

15. Down rush'd beating his wings in vain
the jealous king; his grey brow'd councel-
-lors, thunderous warriors, curl'd veterans.
among helms, and shields, and chariots
horses. elephants: banners, castles, slings
and rocks,

16. Falling, rushing, ruining! buried in
the ruins, on Urthona's dens.

17. All night beneath the ruins, then
their sullen flames faded emerge round
the gloomy king.

18. With thunder and fire: leading his
starry hosts thro' the waste wilderness

he promulgates his ten commands, glancing his beamy eyelids over the deep in dark dismay,

19. Where the son of fire in his eastern cloud, while the morning plumes her golden breast.

20. Spurning the clouds written with curses stamps the stony law to dust, loosing the eternal horses from the dens of night, crying Empire is no more! and now the lion & wolf shall cease.

Chorus

Let the Priests of the Raven of dawn, no longer in deadly black, with hoarse note curse the sons of joy. Nor his accepted brethren whom, tyrant, he calls free; lay the bound or build the roof. Nor pale religious letchery call that virginity, that wishes but acts not!

For every thing that lives is Holy

eternal horses' and is mounted on the back of one as they gallop towards another animal on the ground. The heading 'Chorus' for

the lines celebrating Man's deliverance is flanked by two more splendid horses in violent action. Above the final line the Eagle of Genius is flying upwards with five smaller birds, perhaps the liberated senses, as if to attest to the Holiness of all living things, asserted in the line below:

For every thing that lives is Holy.

The emphasis is on *lives*, for the living Man with his divine and creative Imagination is now equated with God.